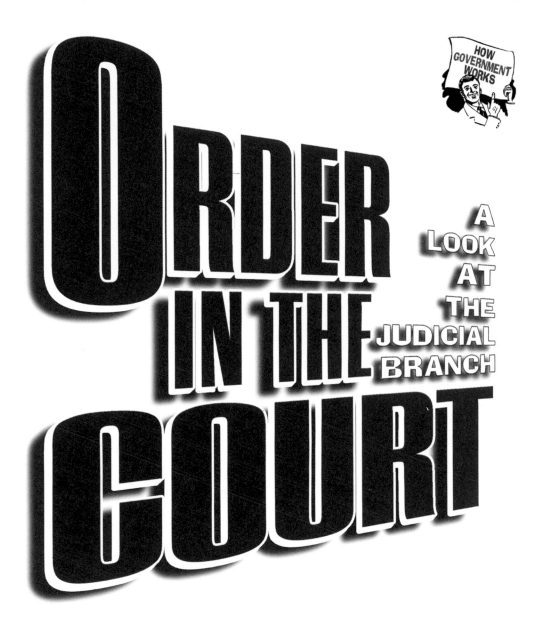

ORDER IN THE COURT

A LOOK AT THE JUDICIAL BRANCH

HOW GOVERNMENT WORKS

By Kathiann M. Kowalski

LERNER PUBLICATIONS COMPANY • MINNEAPOLIS

This book is dedicated to my son, Christopher Michael Meissner

The author gratefully acknowledges the helpful comments offered by Michael Meissner, Laura Meissner, Chris Meissner, Bethany Meissner, Kenneth Moore, and Terrence Perris.

Lerner Publications Company
A division of Lerner Publishing Group
241 First Avenue North
Minneapolis, MN 55401 U.S.A.

Website address: www.lernerbooks.com

Library of Congress Cataloging-in-Publication Data

Kowalski, Kathiann M., 1955–
    Order in the court: a look at the judicial branch / by Kathiann M. Kowalski.
        p.   cm. — (How government works)
    Includes bibliographical references and index.
    Contents: Real-life courtroom dramas — The courts from top to bottom — All the way to the Supreme Court — Crime and punishment — Let's be civil — Your role in the court system.
    ISBN: 0–8225–4698–1 (lib. bdg. : alk. paper)
    1. Courts—United States—Juvenile literature. 2. Judicial power—United States—Juvenile literature. [1. Courts. 2. Judicial power.] I. Title. II. Series.
    KF8700.Z9 K69 2004
    347.73'1—dc21
                                                    2002015767

Manufactured in the United States of America
1 2 3 4 5 6 – DP – 09 08 07 06 05 04

TABLE OF CONTENTS

CHAPTER 1
REAL-LIFE COURTROOM DRAMAS

QUICK QUESTION: Are real-life court cases like the ones on television?

Real-life court cases don't follow a script. They don't wrap up in an hour or two, either. Yet real-life court cases are dramatic, and they affect real people. They can even affect kids. Think about these cases.

School authorities think that a fourteen-year-old girl has been smoking in the bathroom. They find cigarettes and the illegal drug marijuana in her purse. Police arrest the girl. She says that the police should not have been

(Above) Judges, lawyers, and other courtroom personalities appear in both television and real-life court cases.

able to search her purse. The judges of the Supreme Court (the highest court in the country) review the case. They say that the school's search did not go against the girl's rights.

A teenaged boy's website makes fun of his band teacher. The school suspends the boy. But the boy claims the school violated his freedom of speech. He says he will take the case to court. Lawyers settle the case before it goes to court, and the school pays the boy $30,000.

America's courts handle many other cases, too. These cases affect real-life people—people like you!

THE COURTS' JOB: TO INTERPRET LAWS

The courts have a big job. But they do not work alone. Where do they fit into the government?

The answer is in the Constitution. The Constitution is a very important document. It tells how the United States is organized. It limits what the government can do. It guarantees rights for America's people.

The Constitution sets up a federal (national) system of government. Federal laws affect the entire country.

The Constitution tells us how America's government works—including the court system.

Each state also has its own constitution and laws. Counties, cities, and towns have their own laws, too.

Within the federal system, three separate branches share the government's work. The courts—and the judges who work there—form the judicial branch, which is also called the judiciary. The other two branches are called the legislative and the executive branches.

The legislative branch's main job is to make laws. Congress, which is made up of the Senate and the House of Representatives, forms the legislative branch.

The executive branch enforces the laws. Many agencies are part of the executive branch. The president is the head

The most famous courthouse in the United States is the Supreme Court building.

The Federal Bureau of Investigation (FBI) enforces laws. This agency is part of the executive branch.

of the executive branch. This branch also helps define the laws and make them clearer.

When disagreements about the law come up, judges interpret the laws. In other words, they decide what the laws mean. The courts decide real cases. A case may go to court after police arrest someone for a crime or if one person harms another person.

Some court decisions affect many people. Other cases involve only a few. Either way, court decisions affect real people. Sometimes even life and liberty are at stake.

WHAT IS THE LAW?

On television and in real life, courts interpret laws. But just what is the law?

In addition to telling us how the government works, the Constitution is also the nation's highest law. Any law

"SOUND BYTE" "This Constitution . . . shall be the supreme Law of the Land; and the Judges in every State shall be bound thereby, any Thing in the Constitution or Laws of any State to the Contrary notwithstanding."
—from Article VI of the Constitution

that doesn't follow the Constitution is unconstitutional and cannot stand.

Statutes are written laws. Criminal statutes define crimes as acts that harm other people or the community. People who break the law can be put in prison. Someone who breaks a criminal law may also have to pay a fine. Spying on America for another country is a federal crime. Not paying federal taxes is another type of crime. Murder and burglary are examples of state crimes.

Other statutes are called civil statutes. They define rules about business, the environment, health, jobs, and other subjects.

Statutes do not spell out in detail how laws should be carried out. To make the statutes clearer to people, different groups in the executive branch create agency rules. These rules say specifically what people must do to follow statutes. For example, federal statutes say that people must pay taxes. But the Internal Revenue Service (IRS) tells taxpayers exactly which tax forms to fill out. Or the Environmental Protection Agency (EPA) gives businesses details for following statutes about pollution.

Common law is "judge-made law." It develops on a case-by-case basis. When similar cases arise later, judges look at earlier decisions. They try to treat similar cases the same way to make the law consistent. People expect the law to mean the same thing every time.

WHO'S WHO IN THE COURTS?

Like any good drama, America's courts have a cast of characters. Each person plays an important role.

The judge is the official who runs the courtroom. In American courts, the judge is not allowed to take sides. The judge makes sure cases proceed fairly. Judges decide questions of law. In other words, judges decide what the law means.

Judges are the leaders in courtrooms. They listen to the arguments, think about what they've heard, and help decide verdicts.

Why Do People GO TO COURT?

People go to court for many reasons. Here are some common situations:

- Police arrest someone for a crime.
- An auto accident happens.
- A married couple divorces and turns to the court to decide where the children will live or what will happen to the house or other property. Family courts handle these cases.
- A company fires an employee, or the employee feels that the employer is unfair in some way. The employee may sue.
- Someone buys something at a store. The product does not work. The customer may have a right to sue.

Lawyers represent the parties, or the people going to court. Lawyers act as advocates, or legal advisers and helpers. They defend their clients. They argue that their clients are right. Lawyers want the best legal result that they can get for their clients.

The plaintiff is the person who sues, or goes to court for help. In civil cases, the plaintiff is usually a person or company. In criminal cases, the government is always the plaintiff. The government's lawyer in a criminal case is called the prosecutor.

The defendant is the person being sued. The defendant may have to do something, such as pay money or go to jail, if the plaintiff wins.

Each side's lawyers ask witnesses questions. Two main types of witnesses take part in court cases. Fact witnesses have personal knowledge about a case. Expert witnesses have special knowledge about topics in the case. Witnesses must answer truthfully. Their answers, called testimony, become evidence. Documents, items, or other materials can also be evidence. Lawyers use evidence to prove or disprove points in a case.

The jury is a group of regular people who listens to the case. The jury decides questions of fact. This means that jury members weigh the facts in the evidence. They think about what they have heard during the trial. The judge tells them about laws related to the case. Then the jury decides who is innocent and who is guilty according to the laws.

Did You KNOW? Not every case has a jury. If there is no jury, the judge decides questions of both law and fact. He or she decides what the law means and how the law applies to the case.

Sometimes the parties involved in a case accept the jury's decision. Other times, they appeal, or try to have the decision changed in a higher court. An appeal is a claim that the first trial had errors and that another court should hear the case. Appeals courts, or appellate courts, decide if mistakes in the law were made in the first trial. A party who appeals a case hopes that the appeals court will rule differently than the trial court did.

CHAPTER 2
THE COURTS FROM TOP TO BOTTOM

TRUE OR FALSE? The United States has one big court system.

False! The United States has two layers of courts. You can think of them as two separate bus routes. You don't want to get on the wrong bus after school, right? Well, just as each bus takes you to a different place, the federal and state court systems operate separately from each other. Federal courts handle issues that affect the

(Above) This federal courthouse is in Washington, D.C.

whole country. States have their own court systems to handle matters closer to home.

JUDGES RULE!

Judges are trained to decide cases based on their honest judgment about the law. The federal judiciary is independent from the executive and legislative branches. This independence helps the judiciary make fair decisions, without being pressured by the other branches. The Constitution protects this independence.

Personal feelings and interests should not influence judges. A judge's job is steady and secure so the judge can stay fair. In the federal court system, judges hold office "during good behaviour." Basically, judges keep their jobs as long as they want. They do not run for reelection. Neither the president nor Congress can fire federal judges unless a judge does something very wrong, such as commit a crime.

Congress also cannot reduce federal judges' pay while they serve. Judges do not lose money if decisions that they make are unpopular.

Many court decisions are unpopular. In this cartoon, the dog represents income tax. The can tied to his tail represents an unpopular Supreme Court decision about taxes. Bricks representing public disapproval bombard the dog.

A BALANCING ACT

America's founders wanted an independent court system. They also wanted to guard against unlimited power in any one branch of the government. They distrusted a government that was too strong. The Constitution sets up checks and balances to limit federal courts' power. Checks and balances are ways that each government branch can keep the others from getting too much power.

The House of Representatives can impeach (charge) judges who are accused of serious crimes and wrongdoing. If

that happens, the Senate holds a special trial. For a judge to be found guilty, two-thirds of the Senate must vote for conviction. A judge who is convicted loses his or her judgeship.

In 1986 federal judge Harry Claiborne from Nevada was impeached for failing to pay his taxes.

Congress also has a lot to say about how federal courts are run. Congress decides the number of federal court judges. It decides how much money judges get to run the court system.

Congress regulates court jurisdiction, too. Jurisdiction says what kinds of cases a court has the power to decide. Congress can choose to keep some cases out of federal courts. That way, federal judges do not have too much power.

The executive branch also limits courts' power. The president may pardon, or forgive, someone convicted of a federal crime. That keeps courts from punishing people unfairly.

Other important checks come from how federal judges are chosen. Both Congress and the president play a role. The president nominates, or names, people to become judges. The Senate must advise the president and vote on any federal judicial choices.

THE FINAL SAY

The legislative and executive branches of government keep the judiciary branch in check. The courts also keep the other branches of government in check with something called judicial review. Judicial review lets courts interpret laws and decide if they are fair. Court decisions shape the meaning of laws passed by the legislative branch. These decisions also guide the executive branch in enforcing the laws. Ideally, courts' decisions make laws clearer and fairer for everyone.

Judicial review is the courts' most important job. Through judicial review, courts have the last word on America's laws. That protects everyone's rights.

This Senate Judiciary Committee holds hearings to decide on the president's choices for Supreme Court judges.

After nominations the Senate Judiciary Committee (a group of senators who have a say in how the federal courts work) holds hearings. The committee examines the nominated person's background. It questions the person about ethics, or good behavior. The committee considers political issues too.

Next, the committee reports to the entire Senate. Then all senators vote. If the nominee gets a majority (more than half) of the votes, that person is appointed.

A Pyramid of Federal Courts

Think of the federal court system as a pyramid. The United States Supreme Court sits at the top. Its nine judges, called justices, form America's highest court. Almost all of the Supreme Court's cases are appeals from other courts.

Thirteen courts of appeal send cases to the Supreme Court. Twelve hear appeals from specific regions of the country. The U.S. Court of Appeals for the Federal

Circuit hears appeals on special subjects. For example, appeals involving patents (special rights given to inventors) are handled by the U.S. Court of Appeals for the Federal Circuit.

Beneath the courts of appeal are the federal district courts. As of 2003, the United States has ninety-four federal district courts. These courts are general trial courts. Each district covers a geographic area. Every state, plus the District of Columbia and Puerto Rico, has at least one federal district.

A federal district courthouse in Los Angeles, California

Each federal district also has a bankruptcy court. Bankruptcy cases deal with people and companies that cannot pay their debts, or money owed. The U.S. Court of International Trade and the U.S. Court of Federal Claims are other trial courts that deal with special cases. For example, cases seeking money from the federal government go to the claims court.

The Federal Court System

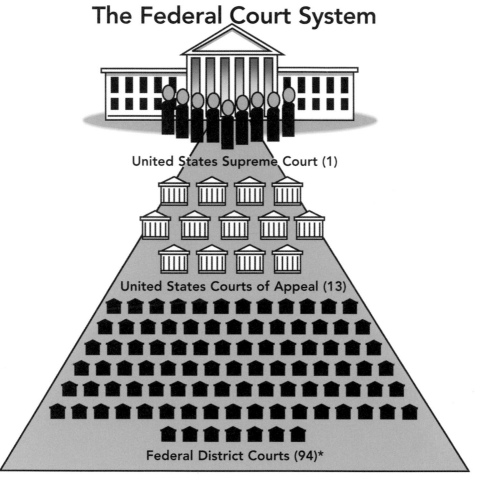

United States Supreme Court (1)

United States Courts of Appeal (13)

Federal District Courts (94)*

*Each federal district court is linked to a bankruptcy court, not shown.

CONSTITUTIONAL CONNECTION

Courts decide if laws follow the Constitution. If a law does not follow the Constitution, it is unconstitutional. The Supreme Court first decided that a law was unconstitutional in 1803. The head of the Supreme Court at that time, Chief Justice John Marshall, wrote, "A law repugnant to the Constitution is void." In other words, any law that goes against the Constitution is no good.

WHAT CASES DO FEDERAL COURTS HEAR?

Not every case belongs in federal court. Federal courts only decide cases over which they have jurisdiction.

"Federal question" jurisdiction covers many cases. It includes cases dealing with the Constitution, federal laws, and international agreements. A case about civil rights could go to federal court. Another federal case might involve a national environmental law.

Federal courts also have "diversity" jurisdiction. Diversity jurisdiction applies if the plaintiffs and defendants in a case come from different states. America's founders were afraid that state courts might side with their own states' residents. So federal courts try these cases instead.

The Constitution says that Congress can limit federal court jurisdiction. For example, Congress has decided that people cannot take their cases to federal court unless a minimum amount of money is at stake. Some cases must start in special "Article I" courts. Those courts handle special subject areas.

LEARN THE LINGO

The United States Tax Court is an Article I court. It handles claims that charge people with not paying enough taxes. Other Article I courts handle cases about the military and benefits for Americans who have fought in wars.

Some cases can only be tried in federal courts, not in state courts. Federal courts have what is called exclusive jurisdiction for those cases. Many other cases can start in either federal or state court.

STATE COURTS

Each of the fifty states has its own court system. Most state court systems have a pyramid structure, just like the federal courts.

Do This!

What is the name of your state's highest court? Check your local library or the Internet to find out the name of your city or county trial court, too.

The highest court in each state system has the last word on state law. Examples of these high courts include the Ohio Supreme Court, the Supreme Judicial Court of Massachusetts, and the New York State Court of Appeals.

A state's general trial courts form the bottom layer. They usually try both civil and criminal cases. States have some special courts, too. One example is family court, which handles divorces and child custody cases. Another example is probate court, which decides issues like what happens to property after someone dies.

Most states have appeals courts between the state's highest court and the general trial courts. These courts hear appeals from the trial courts. States with small populations may let appeals go straight to the state's highest court.

Most state judges serve from four to fourteen years. A few states allow judges to serve for life. Some states let voters

The State Court System

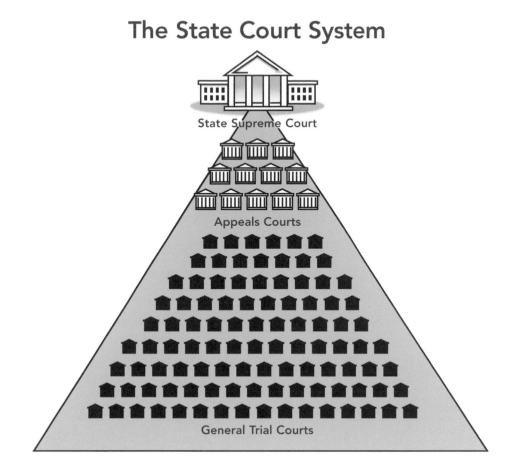

State Supreme Court

Appeals Courts

General Trial Courts

elect judges. Other states let the state's governor appoint judges. A few states let their legislature appoint judges.

Still other states use merit selection. The governor chooses a judge from a list of qualified people. After the judge has served for a while, voters decide whether to keep the judge.

Find out about your state court system by visiting your local or state courthouse. State courts handle most of the criminal and civil cases in America. Those cases often affect you.

CHAPTER 3
ALL THE WAY
TO THE SUPREME COURT

DID YOU KNOW? Being a Supreme Court justice is a seriously long-term job. Supreme Court justices can stay in office for life! The oldest justice ever was Oliver Wendell Holmes, who retired at age ninety. The youngest justice appointed so far was Joseph Story. He joined the Court at age thirty-two.

The United States Supreme Court is America's highest court. The Court's nine justices include the chief justice of the United States, plus eight associate

(Above) **Many important legal decisions have been made at the Supreme Court building in Washington, D.C.**

justices. Together, they have the last word on the Constitution and federal law.

GETTING TO THE SUPREME COURT

"I'll take this case all the way to the Supreme Court!" People say this when they feel very strongly about a case. But getting a case to the Supreme Court is very difficult.

Most Supreme Court cases have already been tried in a lower court. Usually they have also already had an appeal. Cases can come to the Supreme Court from lower federal courts or from states' highest courts.

Do This!

Mark your calendar! The Supreme Court begins each term on the first Monday in October. The term usually ends by early July.

The 2003 Supreme Court was made up of *(top row, left to right)* Justices Ruth Bader Ginsburg, David Hackett Souter, Clarence Thomas, Stephen Breyer, *(bottom row, left to right)* Antonin Scalia, John Paul Stevens, Chief Justice William Hubbs Rehnquist, Sandra Day O'Connor, and Anthony M. Kennedy.

Throughout the year, Supreme Court justices consider petitions for certiorari. These petitions are formal requests for the Court to review a case. If four out of nine justices vote to hear a case, the Court will do so. About 7,500 petitions for certiorari reach the Court each year. In most years, the Court hears only about one hundred cases.

The Court is more likely to hear some cases instead of others. For example, federal laws must work the same way across the nation. So, if a case from one federal appeals court disagrees with another, the Court is more likely to review the case. Does a lower court case misunderstand a previous Supreme Court decision? That increases its chance of being heard, too.

The Supreme Court also prefers cases that affect people beyond just the parties involved in the case. That way the Court shapes law for the entire country. A student drug-testing case, for example, does not affect just one student and one school. It can affect students across the country.

In rare cases, lawsuits can start in the Supreme Court. This may include cases that are between people or groups from two or more states.

DIG DEEPER Since 1789 the Supreme Court has started fewer than two hundred cases. One example was a 1998 case that ruled that New Jersey and New York each owned part of Ellis Island.

HOW THE SUPREME COURT DECIDES CASES

Once the Supreme Court decides to hear a case, both sides' lawyers send legal papers, called briefs, to the Court. These papers discuss each side's legal arguments.

The Court hears spoken arguments on cases. Each side gets thirty minutes. Lawyers plan their talks carefully. They stress their strongest points.

Lawyers rarely say everything they plan to. Often the Supreme Court justices interrupt. They question each side's arguments. They ask about the possible effects of a decision. The sessions are very lively.

LEARN THE LINGO

Amicus curiae legal papers tell the court how a decision could affect people beyond just the case's parties. The Latin phrase means "friend of the court."

Later in the week, the justices meet in private. They discuss the cases and the briefs. Then they vote. For a case to win,

Court sessions can be exciting, but some of the work that justices do behind the scenes isn't much fun. In this cartoon, Supreme Court justices are nearly buried by a pile of cases marked "important," freshly delivered from the lower courts.

more than half of the Court's justices have to vote for it to win. When all nine justices take part, five of the justices must agree.

Often the Court publishes a written opinion about its decision. A member of the winning side writes the majority opinion. All the justices get to read the majority opinion before the Court's decision is final.

Sometimes a justice agrees with the outcome. But the justice may reach his or her decision for reasons besides those in the majority opinion. That justice may write a concurring opinion that gives his or her own reasons for agreeing with the case's outcome.

Sometimes a justice on the losing side writes a dissenting opinion. The dissent says why the justice feels the majority is wrong. Those opinions are read by all the justices. Other justices may join in the dissent. Sometimes, dissents have even persuaded justices to change their votes before the ruling is final.

Finally, the Court announces its decision. The Supreme Court may uphold or reverse a lower court's ruling. The Supreme Court may also send a case back to the lower court for more consideration.

DIG DEEPER Want to be a Supreme Court justice? Do your English homework! In addition to knowing a lot about the law, justices need to be good writers. They have to be able to express their opinions clearly and convincingly.

The Supreme Court publishes all its written opinions—majority, concurring, and dissenting. Written opinions let everyone, including regular citizens, know the justices' reasons for their decisions. They give guidance to the legislative and executive branches.

FAMOUS SUPREME COURT JUSTICES

More than one hundred people have served as justices on the United States Supreme Court. Meet a few of the Court's famous justices.

John Jay (1745–1829) was the United States' first chief justice. Before the Constitution became law, Jay also helped write *The Federalist,* a series of essays in favor of the Constitution.

John Marshall (1755–1835) served as chief justice from 1801 until 1835. Many of Marshall's decisions interpreted the Constitution to favor a strong national government.

Louis Brandeis (1856–1941) became the first Jewish person on the Supreme Court in 1916.

William Howard Taft (1857–1930) served as president of the United States before he was appointed to be chief justice of the United States.

Earl Warren (1891–1974), a former California governor, became chief justice of the United States in 1953. The Warren Court made important rulings on civil rights and criminal defendants' rights.

Thurgood Marshall (1908–1993) became the Supreme Court's first African American justice in 1961.

Byron White (1917–2002) is the only Supreme Court justice in the Pro Football Hall of Fame. "Whizzer" White played for the Pittsburgh Steelers and the Detroit Lions.

Sandra Day O'Connor (b. 1930) became America's first female Supreme Court justice in 1981.

CAN THE SUPREME COURT CHANGE ITS MIND?

Except for additions and changes called amendments, the Constitution's words stay the same. But when the Supreme Court considers new cases, justices think about the ways that people and communities change. This means that constitutional law also changes over time.

In 1940 the Supreme Court ruled that public schools could make students say the "Pledge of Allegiance." People practicing the Jehovah's Witnesses faith disagreed. They believed they could not pledge allegiance to anything or anyone but God.

A Supreme Court case in 1940 took a look at a law requiring schoolchildren to pledge allegiance to the U.S. flag every morning before classes began.

The Jehovah's Witnesses lost the 1940 case. But Justice Harlan Stone wrote a strong dissent. The First Amendment to the Constitution guarantees freedom of religion. Stone said that the government should not make children act against their religious beliefs.

LEARN THE LINGO

Every court case gets its own name. The first piece of the name is the prosecuting party's name. The second piece is the defending party's name. These two names are separated by "v.," which stands for "versus" (against).

West Virginia State Board of Education v. Barnette was a case that went to the Supreme Court in 1943. It also challenged a law that required students to say the "Pledge of Allegiance." But this time, the Court said schools could not make children say the "Pledge of Allegiance" if it went against their beliefs.

What about the 1940 case? The Court said its earlier interpretation of the Constitution had been wrong. *Barnette* overruled the earlier case.

The Court also has changed its views on racial segregation, the separation of people based on their race. During the 1800s, the Court allowed racial segregation in public transportation, such as buses. Court decisions in the 1900s overruled those cases. Racial segregation in schools and other public places is unconstitutional.

CHAPTER 4
CRIME AND PUNISHMENT: CRIMINAL LAW

THINK ABOUT IT: The Constitution guarantees everyone a right to the assistance of counsel. This means that everyone—even people who are accused of awful crimes—deserves to have a lawyer who will do his or her best to win the case. If you were a lawyer, do you think you would take such a person's case?

The United States' founders felt that all people deserved a fair trial, no matter what crime they were accused of. "It is better that ten guilty persons escape than that one innocent suffer," English legal scholar

(Above) This prison in California houses people who have been convicted of crimes.

William Blackstone said more than two hundred years ago. America's courts treat criminal defendants as innocent until they are proven guilty.

WHAT IS A CRIME?

A crime is an act that harms people or communities. Crimes may break state law, federal law, or both. Felonies are the most serious crimes. Murder, kidnapping, and robbery are examples of felonies. Misdemeanors, such as littering or minor vandalism, are less serious crimes.

Under our Constitution, criminal defendants deserve fair treatment. Laws must clearly say what actions are considered crimes. Laws that are too vague are unconstitutional.

The Constitution also forbids ex post facto, or "after the fact" laws. Laws must define a crime *before* the government can punish someone for that crime. Criminal laws that single out one person or one group are also unconstitutional.

The Fifth Amendment to the Constitution says no one can "be deprived of life, liberty, or property, without due process of law." This means that the government cannot just lock someone up, even if police think that the person committed a crime. The government must follow certain rules and allow a fair trial.

DIG DEEPER The Fourth, Fifth, Sixth, and Eighth Amendments all protect criminal defendants' rights. The Fourteenth Amendment makes the states — along with the federal government—respect these rights.

DO YOU HAVE A WARRANT?

Police enforce the laws. When laws are broken, police need to solve crimes. Police must also respect people's rights.

The Fourth Amendment forbids "unreasonable searches and seizures." Usually, police need a warrant (a type of court order) to search a person or his or her property or to take anything from that person.

Some searches without warrants are allowed. Suppose a police officer thinks someone is dangerous or about to commit a crime. Reasonable suspicion lets the officer frisk (search) that person for a weapon.

What if police violate the Fourth Amendment? Then the exclusionary rule applies. This rule says that, at trial, the government cannot use evidence that it got from an illegal search. Police want to convict guilty people. So the rule makes unlawful police action less likely to happen.

YOU ARE UNDER ARREST

Police must give the Miranda warning when arresting someone. Giving the Miranda warning is also called reading the suspect his or her rights. The warning protects the Fifth Amendment right against self-incrimination. That means that the government cannot make a person say things that might damage his or her case. Police cannot force someone to admit committing a crime. If police violate a defendant's Miranda rights, the government cannot use that defendant's statements at trial.

The Miranda warning also talks about the defendant's Sixth Amendment right to a lawyer. If someone cannot afford a lawyer, the court provides one free of

"SOUND BYTE" "You have the right to remain silent. If you choose not to exercise this right, anything you say can and will be used against you in a court of law."
—from the Miranda warning

Police are required to recite the Miranda warning to every person they arrest before taking them to jail.

charge. A defendant may ask to have a lawyer present during police questioning.

A defendant has the right to know what crime he or she is accused of. Police need either a warrant or probable cause for an arrest. Probable cause means that the police must have good reason to think that someone committed a crime.

YOU ARE UNDER ARREST

Within one or two days, police must bring the defendant into court for an arraignment. The arraignment is a process during which the court makes sure that the defendant knows his or her rights.

At arraignment the court formally reads charges against the defendant. In response, the defendant tells the court his or her plea. A plea of "not guilty" means that the defendant

At this arraignment, actor Robert Downey Jr. *(right)* faces two felony drug charges.

denies committing the crime. "Not guilty by reason of insanity" means the defendant admits doing the act. However, the defendant claims he or she could not tell right from wrong at the time. At trial the defendant must prove this defense.

The court rules on bail. Bail is money that a defendant pays to stay out of jail until trial. The court refunds the money if the person shows up for trial. The Eighth Amendment forbids excessive bail. Setting a bail that is excessive (too high) would be a way of punishing someone without a trial.

Not every defendant gets bail. In a murder case, the court may think the defendant is too dangerous to be free. Or he or she may seem likely to run away.

Does the government have enough evidence to go to trial? Pretrial hearings, which may happen before or after arraignment, answer this question. If too little evidence exists against the defendant, the government cannot make him or her face a trial. The defendant's lawyer also receives copies of reports describing the evidence. This exchange of documents is called discovery.

ARE PLEA BARGAINS A BARGAIN?

Less than 10 percent of criminal cases ever get to trial. Most defendants do something called plea bargaining. Defendants who plea-bargain must plead either guilty or nolo contendere (no contest).

A plea-bargaining defendant loses the right to a trial. But, in return, he or she gets a less severe punishment. Plea bargains let defendants get reduced sentences, or lighter punishments. Yet plea bargains remove the risk of a not guilty verdict at trial. Plea bargains make sure that defendants get some punishment.

Did You KNOW? Have you noticed that many modern legal terms—such as ex post facto and nolo contendere—are in Latin? Latin was the language used in ancient Rome. Until several hundred years ago, Latin was still used by educated people in Europe for many official actions.

ON TRIAL

The Sixth Amendment guarantees every criminal defendant a speedy and public trial by jury. Speedy means reasonably soon after arrest.

During trial a defendant has the right to see and hear the witnesses. People cannot testify in secret against a defendant. A defendant also has the right to make witnesses testify in the case. Courts issue subpoenas, or orders to appear in court, to witnesses. Disobeying a subpoena could land someone in jail.

After all the evidence has been presented, lawyers make closing arguments. They explain to the jury how the evidence fits together to support their case. The judge instructs the jury about the law. Then the jury meets in private. Its members deliberate, or consider, the case.

In general, a jury in a criminal case must give a unanimous verdict, or decision. That means that all jurors must agree. The jury can find a defendant guilty only if the government proves guilt "beyond a reasonable doubt." This is a very high burden of proof. The burden of proof is the level of evidence needed to win a case. So, in a criminal case, the prosecutor needs strong evidence to win. The jury must feel very certain that the defendant is guilty.

SENTENCING AND APPEALS

During sentencing the judge says what a guilty person's punishment will be. Prisons do not have to be comfortable, and their rules can be very strict. But under the Eighth Amendment, prisons must meet basic conditions for prisoners' health and safety. Punishment cannot be "cruel and unusual."

During sentencing the convicted party appears before a judge.

About one-third of all defendants who are found guilty appeal the verdicts in their cases. An appeal does not try the whole case again. The appeals court reviews the case record. It reads the case's legal briefs and hears lawyers' arguments.

If the lower court made a legal mistake, the appeals court decides if the error affected the outcome. If the court finds only "harmless error," it lets the conviction stay the same.

If the appeals court thinks that an error made by the lower court during trial might have changed the outcome, it reverses the conviction. Often, the defendant gets a new trial. In other cases, the government can no longer prove its case. For example, the government may be unable to use a confession that it got illegally. Then the defendant goes free.

If the conviction stands, a defendant may try more appeals. States' highest courts may not have to hear all appeals. And the United States Supreme Court chooses which cases to hear.

Courts FOR KIDS

What if a child commits a crime? Every state has a court system for young people, called juvenile court. Why are children treated differently? Punishment is not the purpose of juvenile court. Juvenile courts want to rehabilitate defendants. In other words, they want young people who have broken the law to learn how to be adults who follow the law.

What if a child's crime is a murder? Most states have rules that let the adult courts take over certain cases. Some people say that adult rules are the only fair way to handle cases for school shootings or other awful crimes. Other people say that all young defendants should be protected and rehabilitated. What do you think?

CHAPTER 5
LET'S BE CIVIL: CIVIL LAW

DID YOU KNOW? In exciting television shows, most court cases involve crimes like murder, kidnapping, or stealing. But in real life, many court cases do not involve a crime at all. These cases are called civil cases. Civil cases usually involve conflicts among people or companies. But no one has actually broken the law.

(Above) A lawyer presents evidence to a witness in a civil case. The lawyer's client, a professional hockey player, claims that he was forced to play on an injured ankle and that this treatment ended his career early.

For example, suppose one car crashes into another at a busy intersection. One driver says the other driver was not as careful as he or she should have been. That driver sues the other driver.

Suppose someone gets fired from a job. That person believes the reason he or she was fired was discrimination based on race, age, or gender. The person sues his or her employer.

These are just a couple of situations that produce civil lawsuits. How do courts resolve these conflicts?

BEFORE THE TRIAL

Legal actions (lawsuits) for civil cases start with a complaint. The complaint states the reason for a lawsuit. The person filing the complaint is called the plaintiff.

The person who is being sued is called the defendant. A defendant must respond to the complaint or lose the case. The defendant may file an answer, which deals point by point with the complaint. Or, the defendant can make a motion. For example, a motion to dismiss says the plaintiff could not win even if the plaintiff's claims were the true facts. A defendant might also make his or her own claims against the plaintiff or others.

Discovery comes next. In a civil case, discovery takes more time than it does in criminal cases. Discovery lets each side learn about the other side's case. This step avoids unfair surprises at trial. In general, people must promise that their discovery responses are true and complete.

Depositions are a type of discovery. In depositions witnesses answer lawyers' questions without the judge or jury present. They answer under oath, which means that they have promised

LEARN THE LINGO

Quit complaining! If you were a lawyer, complaints would actually be a big part of your job. Lawyers usually write complaints for their clients.

to tell the truth. A court reporter takes down these answers word for word. Interrogatories are another kind of discovery. Interrogatories ask the plaintiffs and defendants to answer written questions. The two sides exchange documents, too.

The case's lawyers may also file more motions. Sometimes courts decide cases based on motions. Other times parties must wait for trial.

ONE FOR ALL AND ALL FOR ONE

Suppose an airplane crashed because a part did not work correctly. Should every victim's family file a separate lawsuit? Suppose a movie rental chain always charged unfair late fees. Should thousands of customers sue separately?

In cases like these, lawyers often file class action lawsuits. In these cases, one or a few people become plaintiffs for a larger group. People in the larger group must be in similar situations. Their cases must share common facts and legal issues.

Sometimes defendants in a class action suit say there are too many individual issues. If people got hurt, for example, their injuries and medical bills would vary. Defendants may also fear the high cost of class actions. They may want people to sue another way.

DIG DEEPER Have any members of your family been part of a class action? What was the case about? Did they win anything?

But class action lawsuits offer several benefits. They can save time and money. Courts do not have to waste time proving the same facts over and over. Class action lawsuits can provide similar results for all class members. This similarity makes the results fairer.

Ana LeCausi *(left)* was the lead plaintiff in a class action lawsuit against Bridgestone/Firestone Inc. She and the other plaintiffs accused this company of making unsafe car tires, which endangered the lives of people who used them.

Class action lawsuits also let people sue when they might not otherwise be able to afford to. The late movie rental fee case is one example. A few late fees do not justify the costs of suing. But thousands of customers' claims make the case worthwhile.

I'LL SEE YOU IN COURT

Most civil cases never go to trial. Trials are expensive. Often, the parties involved want to avoid paying lawyers and the other costs of a trial. Other times people do not want to take their chances at trial. In most of these cases, the two sides' lawyers work out a settlement, or an agreement, themselves.

Special procedures can help parties reach a settlement. Arbitration is a process that lets parties present a mini-trial to one or more independent lawyers. The lawyers decide who should win. In some cases, called binding arbitration cases, the parties on both sides must accept a panel's decision. In nonbinding arbitration cases, the parties can accept or reject the ruling.

Mediation is another way to settle disagreements. The parties involved hire someone who is not involved in the case—often a lawyer—to help them reach an agreement. The goal is to get a settlement that both sides will accept.

Not all cases can be settled out of court. Those cases go to trial. The plaintiff has the burden of proof in a civil case. This means that the plaintiff must show that his or her claim is more likely true than not. This is easier than the beyond-a-reasonable-doubt burden of proof for criminal cases.

Some civil cases are tried before a judge alone. Others have both a judge and jury. Depending on the court, the jury may or may not have to reach a unanimous verdict. After trial each side has a chance to appeal.

Some courtrooms, such as this one in Texas, are not set up for a jury.

How Would You Decide?

These fictional cases are based on real lawsuits. If you were on the jury, how would you decide?

The Hot Coffee Case

Stella bought hot coffee to go at a fast food restaurant. When she got back in her car, she rested the Styrofoam cup between her legs.

As Stella drove, coffee spilled and burned her legs. She had to go to the hospital. Stella's burns took a year to heal.

Stella sued the fast food restaurant chain. She said the company should not have sold coffee that was hot enough to hurt someone. In the past, hot coffee had burned other customers too.

The restaurant company said that it was not responsible for the accident. It said Stella should have known that the coffee was hot. It said she should not have put the cup where it could spill.

How would you decide?

The Distracted Downhill Skier

A New Hampshire ski resort turned on its snow-making machinery earlier than usual one day. The noise distracted Sarah as she zoomed downhill on her skis. Sarah crashed into a pole. She suffered serious injuries.

Sarah claimed that the resort owners should have warned her about the snow-making machinery. Because they did not, Sarah said the owners should pay for her hospital bills.

The resort owners argued that making snow was part of their business. Skiers should know that the machinery might be operating, they claimed. They also said that skiers should pay attention at all times on the slopes.

How would you decide?

CHAPTER 6
YOUR ROLE
IN THE COURT SYSTEM

TRUE OR FALSE? Kids do not need to know about America's court system.

False! Citizens of all ages should know about how America's court system works.

What role can you play in the court system? Someday you might be the plaintiff or defendant in a lawsuit. You may serve on a jury. You might even become a lawyer or judge. At the very least, you should know how the system works, what your rights are, and what your duties are.

JURY DUTY

Jury duty is both a privilege and a responsibility of American citizenship. Jury duty is a privilege because jurors make decisions that affect real people.

But jury duty is indeed a duty. Jurors (adults serving on a jury) must act impartially. That means they cannot rely on prejudice or personal feelings. They must base their decisions on the facts.

Jurors work hard. They must listen carefully, even if a case takes a long time or gets complicated—or even boring! They must follow court rules to keep decisions fair.

Jurors must listen carefully to everything that happens during a trial. Trials that take many days or weeks can be stressful and tiring for jurors.

Notices that come in the mail tell people when they have jury duty. Sometimes jury duty takes just a day. Sometimes trials last for weeks or months.

Employers must give people time off for jury duty. Some jurors may also get their regular salary. Others get only a modest daily fee from court.

Some people do not have to do jury duty, such as people who are in the army, navy, or other armed services. Other people might put off jury duty until later if serving would cause hardship. For example, someone whose child is very ill may serve at a later time.

Who gets to be a juror? Names are picked from voting lists, licensed driver lists, or both.

Do This!
Look up your local courthouse in the phone book. Call to see if you can visit. You may get a chance to watch a trial.

A federal court juror must be at least eighteen years old and a U.S. citizen. The person must have lived in the judicial district for at least a year. A judicial district can be a state or part of a state. The person must know English. He or she cannot have a mental or physical problem that would interfere with jury duty. Generally, the person cannot have committed a felony. Most state courts have similar rules for selecting jurors.

Some people serve on grand juries. Other people serve on trial juries, or petit juries. (*Petit* means "little" in French.) Trial juries in criminal cases often have twelve jurors. Juries for civil cases have from six to twelve people.

The judge asks potential jurors questions. Lawyers sometimes ask questions too. Does the juror know anyone in the case? Would bias, or personal preference, keep a juror from being fair? If someone's answers suggest a problem, the court does not let that person serve on that case. Usually, lawyers for each side can also turn down one or two jurors if they want.

Sometimes backup jurors hear the case along with the regular jurors. Then, if a juror leaves because of illness or another reason, the trial does not need to be repeated.

The jury selects one juror to read the verdict to the judge and court.

Why go to all this trouble to pick jurors? Jurors' decisions affect their fellow citizens. When jurors act fairly, both sides get a fair trial. People can trust the court system and accept its decisions. And that protects us all.

IS A LEGAL CAREER IN YOUR FUTURE?

Working for justice is a noble goal. Maybe one day you'll be a lawyer or even a judge. To become a lawyer, people generally need a four-year college degree. Next comes law school for three years.

Law schools teach about different legal subjects. Law schools also train students to "think like lawyers." They analyze problems. They research. They learn how to argue cases persuasively.

Law students spend long hours studying.

After law school, lawyers must pass a test called the bar exam. Lawyers who pass the bar exam promise to uphold the state and federal constitutions. They must follow rules about proper ethics, too.

People who become judges have usually worked as lawyers first. Depending on the court, judges may be appointed or elected.

America's court system offers other career opportunities too. Bailiffs and clerks help manage a judge's docket, or list of cases. They also keep order in the courtroom. Court reporters keep accurate records of the proceedings. Technology specialists keep modern courtrooms working smoothly.

KNOW YOUR RIGHTS

Even if you don't choose a legal career, you should know about America's court system. After all, the law affects everyone.

Read newspaper, magazine, and online articles about court cases. Find out how the courts rule on different issues. Those court rulings could affect you.

America's court system is not perfect. Sometimes mistakes mean that criminals go free. Sometimes results are unjust. But many people feel that this is a small price to protect everyone's freedom under the Constitution. The court system tries hard to treat people fairly. It aims to keep innocent people from being convicted. The courts' job is to provide justice for all.

HOLD A MOCK TRIAL

To learn more about America's court system, hold a mock trial. Invite your friends to play different courtroom roles and see what it's like to be part of a court case! For directions visit the following website: <http://www.19thcircuitcourt. state.il.us/bkshelf/resource/ mt_conduct.htm>

GLOSSARY

appeal: a claim that an error was made in a case and that the outcome was wrong. Appeals are heard by appellate courts.

arbitration: one way to reach a settlement. In arbitration, parties present their cases to one or more lawyers before going to trial.

arraignment: a pretrial process during which the court makes sure that the defendant knows his or her rights

burden of proof: the level of evidence needed to win a case

civil lawsuit: a court action for a violation of rights other than a crime. Most civil lawsuits involve claims between individual people.

class action: a lawsuit brought by representatives for a large group

Constitution: the document that explains how the U.S. government is organized. The Constitution also lists the basic rights of American citizens.

defendant: the person who is sued in a civil or criminal lawsuit

deposition: a type of discovery during which witnesses answer lawyers' questions

discovery: a process for parties to learn about each other's case before trial

evidence: information or items that tend to prove or disprove a point in a case

exclusionary rule: a rule that forbids the government from using illegal evidence at a criminal trial

judicial review: the power of the courts to review the actions of other branches and make sure that they agree with the Constitution

judiciary: the court system. The judiciary is also called the judicial branch.

jurisdiction: a court's power to rule on a case

jury: a group of people from the community who review the facts in a court case and reach a decision called a verdict

litigation: lawsuits and other court proceedings

mediation: one way to reach a settlement. In mediation, parties ask a person who is not involved in the case for help coming to an agreement.

Miranda warning: a warning that informs people about constitutional rights when police arrest them

nomination: the naming of someone to fill a post, such as a judgeship

parties: the plaintiffs, defendants, and anyone else named in a case

plaintiff: the person who sues or brings a lawsuit

plea: a defendant's claim of guilt or innocence

plea bargain: a plea of "guilty" or "nolo contendere" in exchange for a lighter sentence

prosecutor: the government's lawyer in a criminal case

rehabilitate: in criminal justice, to change someone who has committed a crime into a citizen who follows the laws

sentence: punishment for a crime

settlement: an agreement among the parties in a case. Cases that are settled do not go to trial.

subpoena: a written order to appear in court

trial: the formal procedure in which a court hears evidence and decides the outcome of a case

verdict: a court's decision on a case

witness: a person with knowledge that affects a court case

SOURCE NOTES

For quoted material: pp. 8, 31, *World Book Encyclopedia*, 2000 ed., s.v. "Constitution of the United States"; p. 14, "American Foreign Policy and the International Criminal Court," *U.S. Department of State*, May 6, 2002, <http://www.state.gov/p/9949.htm> (January 17, 2003); p. 19, *Marbury v. Madison*, 5 US 137 (1803); p. 30, "7341. Blackstone, William. The Columbia World of Quotations," *Bartleby.com: Great Books Online*, n.d., <http://www.bartleby.com/66/41/7341.html> (January 22, 2003); p. 32, "The Miranda Warning," *The United States Constitution Online*, n.d., <http://www.usconstitution.net/miranda.html> (January 22, 2003).

SELECTED BIBLIOGRAPHY

Administrative Office of the United States Courts. "The Federal Judiciary." *U.S. Courts.* n.d. <http://www.uscourts.gov> (July 1, 2002).

———. "Understanding the Federal Courts." *U.S. Courts.* n.d. <http://www.uscourts.gov/understand02/media/UFC99.pdf> or <http://www.uscourts.gov/understand02> (July 1, 2002).

American Bar Association Division for Media Relations and Public Affairs. "Facts about the American Judicial System." *American Bar Association.* 1999. <http://www.abanet.org/media/factbooks/judifact.pdf> (July 1, 2002).

Bardes, Barbara A., Mack C. Shelley II, and Steffen W. Schmidt. *American Government and Politics Today: The Essentials,* 1994–1995 ed. Saint Paul, MN: West Publishing Company, 1994.

Burns, James MacGregor, et al. *Government by the People,* 18th ed. Upper Saddle River, NJ: Prentice Hall, 2000.

Carp, Robert A., and Ronald Stidham. *Judicial Process in America,* 3rd ed. Washington, D.C.: Congressional Quarterly Press, 1996.

Jensen, Bryce A. "From Tobacco to Health Care and Beyond: A Critique of Lawsuits Targeting Unpopular Industries." *Cornell Law Review,* September 2001: 1334.

Melusky, Joseph Anthony. *The American Political System: An Owner's Manual.* Boston: McGraw-Hill, 2000.

O'Brien, David M. *Constitutional Law and Politics: Struggles for Power and Governmental Accountability,* vol. I. 4th ed. New York: W. W. Norton & Co., 2000.

Porto, Brian L. *May It Please the Court: Judicial Processes and Politics in America.* New York: Longman, 2001.

Rehnquist, William H. *The Supreme Court.* New York: Alfred A. Knopf, 2001.

Rutherford, Denny G. "Lessons from Liebeck: QSRs Cool the Coffee." *Cornell Hotel & Restaurant Administration Quarterly,* June 1998: 72.

Supreme Court of the United States. n.d. <http://www.supremecourtus.gov> (July 1, 2002).

Weinreb, Lloyd L. *Leading Constitutional Cases on Criminal Justice.* New York: Foundation Press, 2001.

FURTHER READING AND WEBSITES

American Bar Association.
Website: <http://www.abanet.org>
Check out this site for all kinds of information about being a law student or a lawyer.

Aria, Barbara. *The Supreme Court.* New York: Franklin Watts, 1994.

Ben's Guide to U.S. Government for Kids.
Website: <http://bensguide.gpo.gov>
Your guide, Ben Franklin, introduces you to all areas of the government, including how laws are made and how the branches of government work together.

C-Span.
Website: <http://www.cspan.org>
This fact-packed news site is your source for breaking stories on court cases and other legal matters.

Inside the Courtroom: Department of Justice (DOJ) USA Web Site for Kids.
Website: <http://www.usdoj.gov/usao/eousa/kidspage/index.html>
Learn about the law from lawyers themselves. This site covers cases, legal terms, and more.

Kelly, Zachary A. *Our Court System.* Vero Beach, FL: Rourke Corporation, 1993.

Pascoe, Elaine. *America's Courts on Trial: Questioning Our Legal System.* Brookfield, CT: Millbrook Press, 1997.

Quiri, Patricia Ryon. *The Supreme Court.* New York: Children's Press, 1999.

Summer, Lila, and Samuel G. Woods. *The Judiciary: Laws We Live By.* Austin, TX: Raintree Steck-Vaughn, 1993.

Supreme Court of the United States.
Website: <http://www.supremecourtus.gov>
This site is your source for Supreme Court news and information.

U.S. Courts.
Website: <http://www.uscourts.gov>
Check here for an overview of the U.S. courts, from bankruptcy and district courts all the way to the Supreme Court.

Weizmann, Daniel. *Take a Stand! Everything You Ever Wanted to Know about Government.* Los Angeles: Price Stern Sloan, 1996.

INDEX

ABOUT THE AUTHOR

Kathiann M. Kowalski has spent fifteen years practicing law. She holds a bachelor's degree in political science from Hofstra University. She received her law degree from Harvard Law School, where she was a member of the *Harvard Law Review*. Ms. Kowalski's books for young people include *Campaign Politics: What's Fair? What's Foul?* and *Hazardous Waste Sites*.

PHOTO ACKNOWLEDGEMENTS

The photographs in this book are reproduced with the permission of, © Dennis MacDonald/Photo Network, pp. 4, 9, 44; National Archives, p. 5; Corbis Royalty Free Images, pp. 6, 22, 42, 45, 47; © Bettmann/CORBIS, pp. 14, 25, 28; © 2003 Jay Mallin, pp. 12, 16; © CORBIS, p. 13; © Steve Starr/ CORBIS, p. 17; Diagrams by Bill Hauser, pp. 18, 21; Collection, The Supreme Court Historical Society, p. 23; © Photo Network, p. 30; © T. J. Florian/Photo Network; AP/Wide World Photos, p. 34, 38; © Mikael Karlsson, p. 36; © Reuters NewMedia Inc./CORBIS, pp. 41, 7; © Ed Eckstein/CORBIS, p. 48.